John Peacock

Fashion Sourcebooks The 1940s

With 329 illustrations

Thames and Hudson

For Ray Holman

© 1998 Thames and Hudson Ltd,
London

British Library Cataloguing-
in-Publication Data
A catalogue record for this book is
available from the British Library.

ISBN 0-500-28041-X

Printed and bound in Slovenia
by Mladinska Knjiga

Contents

Introduction   7

The Plates

1940   9

1941   13

1942   17

1943   21

1944   25

1945   29

1946   33

1947   37

1948   41

1949   45

Descriptions   49

Chart of the Development of 1940s Fashion   60
Biographies of Designers   62
Sources for 1940s Fashion   64
Acknowledgments   64

Women's fashion in the 1940s divides into two separate parts: from 1940 to 1946, and from early 1947 to the end of the decade. The first part was dominated by the Second World War. Dress, echoing military uniforms, was consciously and almost wholly utilitarian. In the United Kingdom, rationing came into effect in the summer of 1941 and the following year saw the introduction of the Utility Clothing Scheme which restricted among other things the amount of cloth that could be used in garments, the maximum length and width of a skirt, and the number of pleats, buttons and trimmings. These limitations gave rise to simple designs that were well-cut, well proportioned and stylish, usually in the form of jackets or dresses with square, padded shoulders and straight, knee-length skirts. In the United States similar restrictions were imposed, though for a shorter time than in the United Kingdom. American designers, also constrained by rationing, began to use alternative fabrics in new and inventive ways. In both the US and the UK, the experience gained in the speedy mass production of uniforms, and in economical cutting and use of cloth led to more scientific and better mechanized methods of large-scale production in the clothing trade.

Wartime shortages were often a spur to creativity. Though women who were involved in war work were likely to wear almost anything, fashionable or not, so long as it was functional and fitted the occasion, attempts were made to brighten up the utilitarian look with frivolous little hats which were often concocted from raffia, ribbon, curtain fabric or even paper and men's silk neckties. Old straw and felt hats were expertly remodelled and trimmed with feathers or homemade silk flowers. Brightly coloured, boldly patterned silk headscarves, bound around the head in the form of a turban, were immensely popular.

Paris, traditionally the world's most powerful force in fashion, lost much of its influence due to wartime isolation. But in 1947 it came back with a bang. On 12 February of that year the French couturier Christian Dior launched his 'Corolle line', instantly nicknamed 'The New Look' – the most famous and controversial collection any designer has ever produced. The New Look was not in fact new – a number of Parisian designers had shown similar lines in the years immediately preceding the war – but it was ultra-feminine and grandly extravagant, and arriving as it did so soon after the war, when some rationing and restrictions were still in force, it caused a sensation. The old pre-1947 lines were demolished at a stroke. Luxurious and romantic, the Corolle line was lavish in its use of fabric, trim and detail. Day dresses had mid-calf-length billowing skirts, narrow waists, lightly padded hips and bosoms, narrow rounded shoulders and every hard edge softened. Even the smart tailored suit with its long jacket was moulded over a padded lining and teamed with a pencil-slim skirt which was only twelve inches from the ground. The look was finished with a new fashion accessory: a slender rolled umbrella with a long, elegant handle.

The New Look called for new physical features: rounded shoulderlines meant the discarding of the bulky shoulder pads that had previously been worn with every garment; rounded bosoms and tiny waists required new-style underwear and corsets; the fuller, wider skirts needed layers of flounced and stiffened petticoats.

Men's fashions during the 1940s were relatively stationary and somewhat dull, dominated as they were by military uniform. In consequence they require fewer illustrations than women's. The types of clothes worn by men during this period as well as the basic trends have been shown, on average, with one example on each page.

In the main, the fashions I have used are such as would have been worn by men and women of the middle or upper-middle classes and by people who, while not necessarily being 'dedicated followers of fashion', would have had a keen interest in the latest styles. The sources from which I have drawn – chiefly from Great Britain, North America and France – include contemporary magazines, catalogues and journals; museum collections; original dated photographs and my own costume collection. This Sourcebook is divided into ten sections, each of which includes four subdivisions covering Day Wear, Evening Wear (alternately on two occasions, Wedding Wear), Sports and Leisure Wear and a section on either Underwear or Accessories. Following the main illustrations are ten pages of schematic drawings accompanied by detailed notes about each example, giving particulars of colour, fabric, cut and trimming as well as accessories and other useful information.

Then follow two pages of drawings which illustrate the decade 'at a glance' and which demonstrate the evolution of the period and its main development trends.

Biographies of the most important international fashion designers of the decade are also included as well as a list of further reading suggestions into the styles of this period.

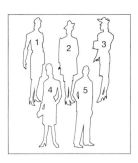

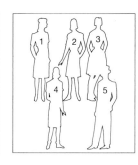

1940 Day Wear

1 Mustard-yellow wool dress, V-shaped neckline to above high top-stitched yoke seam, gathered shaping from shoulders and neck point, centre-front seam from under yoke to hem of knee-length flared skirt, seam top-stitched from yoke to above hip-level, gathered shaping at each side, inset waistband, side fastening, elbow-length sleeves, padded shoulders. Brimless brown felt hat, silk cord trim. Brown suede gloves. Fur muff. Brown suede shoes, self-fabric roll trim, high heels. **2** Three-quarter-length fawn imitation-fur collarless coat, single-breasted fastening from above waist to under V-shaped neckline, large brown plastic buttons, hip-level welt pockets, full-length sleeves, padded shoulders. Brown wool skirt. Fawn felt hat, tiny crown, flat top, brown ribbon trim, curled brim. Brown leather gloves; matching shoes. **3** Blue-grey wool two-piece jumper suit: fly fastening from hem to under high collar, self-fabric buckled belt, long inset sleeves, padded shoulders, angled chest-level piped pockets; knee-length skirt, pleated front panel. Grey felt hat, black ribbon band, red feather trim. Black leather bag; matching gloves and shoes, high lace-up vamps, high heels. **4** Pink wool-crepe dress, bloused bodice, high round neckline, gathered shaping from curved yoke seams, matching hip panels and pockets in knee-length flared skirt, three-quarter-length sleeves, narrow cuffs, padded shoulders, narrow self-fabric buckled belt. Pale-grey felt hat, blue velvet ribbon trim. Pink suede gloves. Grey wool clutch bag, blue plastic clasp top. Blue leather shoes, bow trim, high heels. **5** Two-piece dark-grey wool suit: single-breasted jacket, three-button fastening, flap pockets; straight-cut trousers, turn-ups. Blue and white striped cotton shirt, plain white collar. Blue and grey striped silk tie. Black leather lace-up shoes.

Evening Wear

1 Two-piece black wool evening suit: double-breasted jacket, wide lapels faced with black silk, hip-level piped pockets, breast pocket, white silk handkerchief; straight-cut trousers, no turn-ups. White cotton shirt. Black silk bow-tie. Black patent-leather lace-up shoes. **2** Deep-blue fine wool-crepe evening dress, low V-shaped neckline, ruched shaped side panel of self-fabric from hip-level to under deep scooped armholes, slender bodice and skirt cut in flared panels, no waist seam. Silver kid strap sandals. **3** Black silk-jersey dinner dress, full-length inset sleeves, narrow shoulder yoke, padded shoulders, fitted bodice, ankle-length flared skirt, narrow belt, clasp fastening, shaped neckline, pleated front panels of bodice and skirt in yellow-gold tissue; matching turban hat with large bow trim on one side. Black suede shoes, peep toes. **4** Full-length silk-taffeta evening dress, fitted bust-length top in royal-blue, wide square neckline, brooch trim at each point, short inset sleeves, padded shoulders, matching band of royal-blue on hem of pale-violet skirt, gathered from hip seam, skirt matches lower fitted bodice from under bustline to hip-level. **5** Fine black wool dinner dress, bloused bodice, V-shaped neckline, gathered shaping from asymmetric inset band above bust, black sequined embroidered motif, three-quarter-length inset sleeves, ruched detail above hems, full-length skirt, gathered front panel from hip-level seam. Black and grey fox-fur stole. Black satin strap sandals.

Sports and Leisure Wear

1 Holiday wear. Dress in white linen patterned in red, bloused bodice from above wide shaped inset band, collar and wide lapels, short puff sleeves, padded shoulders, knee-length gathered skirt. Small white straw hat, shallow crown, red ribbon trim; hat worn with red open-mesh cotton snood. White canvas shoes, peep toes. **2** Tennis. Knee-length white linen dress, fly fastening from under collar to hip-level, tuck to hem of flared skirt, bloused bodice, welt pockets at chest-level, short sleeves, padded shoulders, self-fabric belt, large hip-level patch pockets, flaps from under belt. White leather shoes, bow trim, wedge heels. **3** Beach wear. Blue and white striped cotton sundress, wide plain white cotton shoulder straps matching bindings of shaped neckline and centre-front button-fastening through to hem and trim on angled hip-level shaped patch pockets, knee-length skirt gathered from waist. Blue canvas sling-back shoes, peep toes, high wedge heels. **4** Tennis. White cotton two-piece jumper suit: hip-length collarless top, self-fabric buckled belt, high round neckline, two small patch pockets with buttoned flaps, one on bustline, the other above, short inset sleeves, padded shoulders; knee-length box-pleated skirt. White cotton ankle socks. White canvas slip-on shoes. **5** Holiday wear. Single-breasted beige linen-tweed jacket, three-button fastening, patch pockets, narrow lapels. Straight-cut light-brown flannel trousers with turn-ups. Cream cotton collar-attached shirt. Blue and brown cotton tie. Natural straw trilby, high crown, blue petersham ribbon band, narrow brim turned up at back. Light-tan leather lace-up shoes.

Underwear and Negligee

1 Maroon-red wool dressing gown, front panels of fitted bodice and full-length flared skirt cut in one piece without waist seam, button-through fastening from under wide sweetheart neckline to mid-calf-level, self-fabric covered buttons, half-belt set into side panel seams, tied at back, full-length fitted sleeves, padded shoulders. **2** Pink cotton unstructured brassiere, cups shaped with darts, ribbon shoulder straps, back fastening. Pink cotton-satin knickers, wide legs, scalloped hems, side-hip button fastening. **3** Pale-green satin slip, darted bust shaping in V-shaped panels, neck edge trimmed with fine lace pleating, satin ribbon shoulder straps, knee-length flared skirt. Green velvet mules, green satin bow trim, high heels. **4** Sage-green cotton dressing gown finely checked in grey, wrapover front and shawl collar piped in plain grey cotton matching turned-back cuffs of full-length inset sleeves, edges of tie-belt and stitched cuffs on patch pockets. Green and white striped cotton pyjamas. Black leather house slippers. **5** Red and black striped taffeta housecoat, collarless wrapover front, narrow shoulder yoke, full-length inset sleeves gathered into narrow cuffs, padded shoulders, wide waist sash, large bow tied on side hip, wide full-length skirt cut in flared panels. **6** Pale-blue silk nightdress, low square neckline edged with pale-coffee lace to match trim on short cap sleeves and hem of full-length flared skirt, skirt and bodice cut in wide panels, no waist seam.

1941 Day Wear

1 Charcoal-grey wool two-piece suit: long single-breasted fitted jacket, three-button fastening, turned-up collar and lapels, seams of top-stitched panels continue into knee-length skirt, hip-level patch pocket, inverted box-pleat, black ribbon bow trim matching small breast pocket, fitted inset sleeves, padded shoulders. Brimless draped black silk hat, pink silk carnation trim. Black leather clutch bag; matching shoes. **2** Powder-blue linen dress, bloused bodice above navy-blue leather buckled belt, matching buttons on mock double-breasted fastening, top-stitched darts on right side of fabric continue as hip yoke in knee-length flared skirt, white cotton-piqué roll collar matching cuffs of short sleeves, padded shoulders. Navy-blue felt hat, small crown, swept-up bonnet brim. Navy-blue leather clutch bag. White cotton gloves. Navy-blue leather shoes. **3** Yellow crepe dress patterned with grey and white flowers, bloused bodice, self-fabric buckled belt, elbow-length sleeves, padded shoulders, gathered shaping between high round neckline and curved half-yoke seams, cut repeated under bustline and on hipline of knee-length skirt, gathered side panels. Small white straw hat, yellow flower trim. White cotton gloves. Black and white leather shoes. **4** Tan and beige patterned wool-jersey edge-to-edge coat, full-length fitted sleeves, padded shoulders, hip-level welt pockets, wide ribbed grey wool-jersey lapels matching buckled belt and collarless dress. Beige felt hat. Long beige leather gloves. Tan leather shoes. **5** Grey wool three-piece suit: single-breasted jacket, three-button fastening, wide lapels, piped pockets; single-breasted collarless waistcoat; straight-cut trousers, turn-ups. White cotton collar-attached shirt. Striped silk tie. Grey felt trilby. Black leather lace-up shoes.

Evening Wear

1 Fine grey wool-crepe dinner dress, bloused bodice, button fastening from above waist-level to under low V-shaped neckline, self-fabric covered buttons, small beaded patch pockets at bust-level, short inset sleeves, padded shoulders, floor-length flared skirt gathers at front from decorative pinafore panel, self-fabric belt tied into bow. Silver kid strap sandals. **2** Dinner ensemble: bright-pink silk-taffeta blouse, wide padded shoulders, shaped epaulette extensions, self-fabric covered button trim, roll collar; full-length black silk-crepe skirt, draped around high waist and over hips, front panel of unpressed pleats. Black satin shoes. **3** Blue, pink and silver flower-patterned fine silk-brocade evening dress, fitted and ruched bodice from low neckline to hip-level, shaped epaulette shoulder straps, floor-length flared skirt. Silver kid shoes, peep toes. **4** Floor-length red velvet evening cape, wide padded shoulders, embroidered and beaded stand collar matching large patch pockets at hip-level. Floor-length black taffeta evening dress. Elbow-length black silk gloves. Black satin strap sandals. **5** Two-piece black wool evening suit: single-breasted fitted jacket, linked-button fastening, wide lapels faced in black satin, hip-level piped pockets, breast pocket with folded white silk handkerchief; straight-cut trousers, no turn-ups, satin ribbon on outside seams. White cotton shirt worn with wing collar. Black satin bow-tie. Black patent-leather lace-up shoes.

Sports and Leisure Wear

1 Casual wear. Short-cropped double-breasted ruby-red wool-tweed jacket, wide lapels, long inset sleeves, padded shoulders. Pale-grey wool-flannel trousers, high waist, wide legs, turn-ups. Oxblood-red leather lace-up shoes, flat heels. **2** Tennis. White cotton shirt, buttoned-strap fastening to under attached long pointed collar worn open, two matching chest-level patch pockets with buttoned flaps, short sleeves, stitched cuffs. White flannel trousers, straight-cut legs, turn-ups, pleats under wide waistband, self-fabric buckled belt, hip-level pockets set into side seams. White leather lace-up shoes. **3** Golf. Single-breasted dark-green wool jacket, single self-fabric covered button under small shawl collar and above wide round stitched neckline seam, one matching button on inset waistband, two below to high hip-level and one on each cuff of long full sleeves, padded shoulders, thigh-length flared skirts. Rust-brown wool trousers, wide legs, turn-ups. Tan leather step-in shoes, fringed tongues, flat heels. **4** Tennis. White cotton dress, wide mock-lapels from centre-front seam, small collar, short sleeves, narrow cuffs, padded shoulders, wide tuck from outside edge of hip-level pockets to hemline of flared knee-length skirt, self-fabric belt, metal clasp fastening. White canvas lace-up shoes, flat heels. **5** Tennis. White linen all-in-one playsuit, single-breasted button fastening from waistline through deep inset waistband to under narrow lapels, small collar, short inset sleeves, stitched cuffs, padded shoulders, short divided skirt, knife-pleat each side centre-front. White canvas lace-up sports shoes, rubber soles and toecaps, flat heels.

Accessories

1 Blue felt hat, front trimmed with checked silk ribbon, narrow brim. **2** Silk turban embroidered with gold sequins. **3** Beret, self-fabric half-bow trim. **4** Cream straw hat, tiny crown, ribbon-and-bow trim, wide flat brim. **5** Red felt hat, small crown, flat top, draped silk band, feather trim, small brim. Silk taffeta scarf. **6** Pink straw hat, silk flower trim. **7** Leather shoes, wide crossed strap fronts, peep toes, high heels. **8** Navy-blue and white leather shoes, perforated detail. **9** White straw hat, tiny crown, flat top, navy-blue ribbon trim split at front, wide brim. **10** Dark-red suede shoes, high tongues, scalloped edges, bow trim. **11** Grey trilby, black band, curled brim. **12** Tan leather shoes, high vamps, stitched detail, high heels. **13** Suede shoes, self-binding and rouleau bow trim, peep toes, high heels. **14** Leather shoes, high tongues, strap-and-buckle fastening, no toecaps. **15** Blue suede monogrammed clutch bag, clasp fastening. **16** Green leather handbag, double rouleau handles, clasp fastening. **17** Fawn trilby, high crown, wide ribbon band, bow trim, wide brim. **18** Tan leather sandals, open sides and front detail, strap-and-buckle fastening. **19** Evening bag, metal frame, clasp fastening. **20** Leather clutch bag, zip fastening in side, fringed leather trim. **21** Brown leather clutch bag, hand top-stitched flap and band. **22** Leather lace-up shoes, no toecaps. **23** Straw hat, wide brim, self-fabric bow trim. **24** Red leather shoes, high tongues, bow trim. **25** Trilby, flat top, brim turned up at back. **26** Wool-tweed golf cap, side sweep to crown, narrow peak. **27** Tiara of pink, white and blue silk flowers. **28** Leather step-in shoes, high tongues, no toecaps. **29** Blue velvet house slippers, self-fabric bow trim. **30** Black velvet hat, trimmed with multicoloured silk flowers.

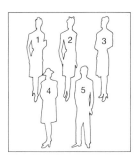

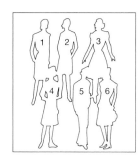

1942 Day Wear

1 Wine-red wool two-piece suit: hip-length edge-to-edge jacket, fastening with loops and buttons in four sets of four from above hemline to under narrow stand collar, self-fabric buckled belt, two inset bands of bias-cut self-fabric from under arms to centre-front at bust-level, full-length tight inset sleeves, padded shoulders; bias-cut knee-length flared skirt. Red silk turban. Black leather envelope clutch bag; matching shoes, lace-up detail, high heels.
2 Two-piece wool jumper suit: long single-breasted turquoise jacket, large hip-level patch-and-flap pockets, upper bodice tucked from above self-fabric tie-belt to under high yoke seam, shirt collar in fawn, matching lapel facings, yoke, full-length sleeves under padded shoulders and knee-length box-pleated skirt. Brown leather shoes.
3 Cherry-red wool dress, semi-fitted bodice above self-fabric belt with covered buckle, knee-length flared panelled skirt, black wool yoke with scalloped top-stitched edges continues over padded shoulders above long sleeves, scalloped pockets set vertically at hip-level into panel seams. Black leather shoes, turned-down tongues, high heels.
4 Knee-length green and blue herringbone wool-tweed coat, single-breasted fastening from waist-level to under wide lapels, large collar, flared from under arm to hem, long raglan sleeves, padded shoulders, hip-level welt pockets, top-stitched edges, raised and top-stitched seams. Blue and green patterned silk scarf. Navy-blue felt hat, small crown, turned-down brim. Navy-blue leather shoes, round toes, high heels. 5 Two-piece blue and grey striped wool suit: double-breasted unfitted jacket, wide lapels, patch pockets, stitched cuffs; wide trousers, turn-ups. White cotton collar-attached shirt. Blue and silver-grey patterned silk tie. Black leather lace-up shoes.

Wedding Wear

1 White silk wedding dress, fitted bodice and full-length skirt cut in flared panels, no waist seam, short train, shaped panels gathered from padded shoulders to under bust each side of V-shaped neckline, tight wrist-length inset sleeves. Pleated white silk-organdie headdress, floor-length silk-tulle veil.
2 Morning suit: single-breasted dark-grey wool morning coat, single-button fastening above waist seam, wide lapels, flower in buttonhole; single-breasted collarless waistcoat in matching fabric; straight-cut black and grey striped wool trousers, no turn-ups. White cotton shirt worn with wing collar. Grey striped silk tie, pearl stud. Dark-grey top hat. Pale-grey suede gloves. Black leather shoes; grey felt spats.
3 Dusty-pink rayon-satin bridesmaid dress, fitted bias-cut bodice from shaped hip seam to matching seam under bust, upper bodice shaped by gathers from padded shoulders to bustline, short inset sleeves, narrow stitched cuffs, spray of fresh flowers worn on one side shoulder, full-length flared skirt. Headdress of tiny pink wax flowers. 4 White silk wedding dress, top-stitched V-shaped neckline matching cuffs of tight full-length inset sleeves, padded shoulders, side bodice fitted from hip-level, gathered bust shaping, central bodice and ground-length skirt cut without waist seam, side skirt gathered from hip seams, short train. Headdress of gathered white satin ribbons, ground-length silk-tulle veil.
5 Oyster rayon-satin wedding dress, round neckline, three-strand pearl necklace, seam under bust, pointed at centre-front, gathered shaping, tight full-length inset sleeves, padded shoulders, lower bodice and ground-length skirt cut without waist seam, diagonal side and hip seams, short train. Headdress of tiny wax flowers, ground-length silk-tulle veil.

Sports and Leisure Wear

1 Tennis. White linen dress, button fastening, small collar, buttoned belt, short inset sleeves, stitched cuffs, piped pockets at bust-level, two decorative panels, one from padded shoulders, one from waist continuing to hip-level in flared skirt, concealed pockets in outer panels, wide unpressed box-pleats. White leather shoes.
2 Tennis. White cotton collar-attached shirt, pointed collar, short inset sleeves, stitched cuffs, patch pocket. White linen pleated shorts, turn-ups, elasticated cotton belt, clasp fastening. White cotton ankle socks. White canvas sports shoes. 3 Holiday wear. Pale-blue cotton blouse, small collar, threaded ribbon fastening matching trim on cuffs of short puff sleeves, padded shoulders. Sleeveless single-breasted checked cotton fitted waistcoat, low scooped neckline, pointed hemline. Knee-length pale-blue cotton gathered skirt, bias-cut band above hemline to match waistcoat. White leather shoes, crossed straps, low wedge heels. 4 Holiday wear. Dark-blue cotton flared pinafore skirt, waistband extended to form shaped bib, wide shoulder straps, self-fabric buckled belt, hip-level patch pockets, mock-buttoned flaps. Red and blue spotted cotton blouse, notched shawl collar, button fastening, elbow-length sleeves, padded shoulders. Red straw hat. Red canvas shoes, peep toes, wedge heels. 5 Country wear. Brown and tan wool-tweed single-breasted jacket, flap pockets, single ticket pocket. Light-brown wool trousers, straight-cut, turn-ups. Brown wool sweater. Patterned silk scarf. Brown trilby. Brown leather shoes. 6 Country wear. Brown and grey tweed dress, small collar, button fastening, padded shoulders, short inset sleeves, stitched cuffs, patch pockets, buttoned belt and flaps, flared skirt, centre-front box-pleat. Brown felt hat. Brown suede gloves; matching shoes.

Underwear and Negligee

1 Hand-quilted black silk-satin dressing gown patterned with multicoloured posies of flowers, wrapover front, wide notched shawl collar, edges piped in plain black satin through to hem of flared skirts, padded shoulders, full-length wide inset sleeves, self-fabric tie-belt, large hip-level patch pockets. 2 Pale-peach-pink rayon slip, fitted bodice and bra top, neckline bordered with pale-cream nylon lace matching hemline of flared skirt, pale satin ribbon shoulder straps. Satin house slippers. 3 Pink silk camisole, fitted bra top, appliqué of cream lace flowers. Knickers in matching fabric, shaped hip yoke, side-button fastening, flared legs, lace flower appliqué on sides. 4 Peach-pink silk-satin camisole patterned with self-colour sprays of flowers, straight neckline edged with pale-coffee lace, fine self-fabric rouleau shoulder straps tied on shoulders. Knickers in matching fabric, flared legs and side pleats edged with lace. Coffee velvet mules, low thick heels. 5 Single-breasted cream wool housecoat, fastening with black wool-covered buttons from knee-level to under rounded shawl collar which narrows to back of neck, fitted bodice and ground-length flared skirts cut in one piece, no waist seam, padded shoulders, black and white striped wool full-length inset bishop-style sleeves gathered into buttoned cuffs.
6 Cream rayon-satin sleeveless nightdress, bloused bodice over drawstring waist, narrow ribbon tie, low V-shaped neckline edged with fine dark-cream nylon lace matching deep armholes, under-bust seaming, seamed decoration over bust and trim on hemline of flared skirt.

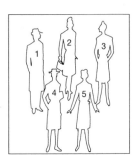

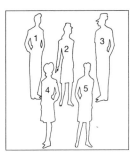

1943 Day Wear

1 Knee-length charcoal-grey wool double-breasted overcoat, wide lapels, diagonal hip-level piped pockets, single breast pocket. Grey flannel trousers, turn-ups. Blue cotton collar-attached shirt. Plain blue wool tie. Dark-grey trilby. Black leather lace-up shoes. 2 Three-piece blue and grey striped wool suit: hip-length semi-fitted edge-to-edge jacket, self-fabric buttoned belt, wide curved lapels, padded shoulders, fitted full-length inset sleeves, collarless top, loop-and-button fastening under white cotton-piqué bow-tie; knee-length flared skirt, two sets of knife-pleats facing centre-front. Navy-blue straw hat, flared topless crown set onto narrow band, brooch trim. Navy-blue leather gauntlet gloves; matching handbag and shoes. 3 Collarless linen dress, red and cream spotted bodice, button fastening under large bow tie, padded shoulders, short inset sleeves, self-fabric buckled belt, pointed half-yoke and floating patch pockets with side openings, plain cream linen knee-length flared skirt. Red leather lace-up shoes, wooden soles and heels. 4 Light-brown and green flecked wool-tweed coat, wrapover front, tie-belt, wide lapels and large collar, gathered shaping under shoulder yoke, padded shoulders, wide full-length inset sleeves, panel seam from yoke to hemline, triangular patch pockets set at an angle at hip-level, button trim, top-stitched edges and detail. Bottle-green silk scarf; matching straw hat. Green leather clutch bag, flap-and-button fastening; matching shoes, low wedge heels, thick soles, wide bar straps. 5 Yellow linen dress, semi-fitted bodice buttoned under collar and revers, padded shoulders, short brown linen inset sleeves matching inset band across bustline with yellow linen rosette trim, self-fabric tie-belt, knee-length flared and panelled skirt. Brown leather shoes.

Evening Wear

1 Mustard-yellow wool-crepe dinner dress, hip-length fitted bodice, centre-front seam ruched from above inset hip-level frill to under high grown-on collar, padded shoulders, full-length fitted sleeves, slightly flared ankle-length skirt. Large yellow silk flower hair decoration. Black fox-fur stole. Black suede shoes, gold kid trim, peep toes. 2 Midnight-blue rayon-crepe dinner dress, collarless cross-over draped bodice from narrow shoulder yoke to under bust seam, padded shoulders, full-length fitted sleeves, narrow ruched inset panel from wrist to above elbow-level, self-fabric tie-belt, ground-length flared skirt, front panel gathered from curved hip yoke. Silver-grey draped silk turban. Silver kid shoes. 3 Ruby-red silk dinner dress, semi-fitted bodice, low V-shaped neckline, bound edges end in bow at point, short inset sleeves, gathered shaping from padded shoulders through self-fabric loops over bust, cut-away triangular panel on each side neck edge to loop, self-fabric tailored belt, ankle-length skirt, unpressed pleats over side hips. Gold kid shoes. 4 Black satin dinner dress, low V-shaped neckline, padded shoulders, full-length inset sleeves, gathered shaping from under bust seam, knotted self-fabric tie on centre-front of seam, ground-length skirt, gathered front panel from shaped hip seam. Black satin shoes. 5 Emerald-green silk dinner dress, fitted bodice, self-fabric covered button trim on centre-front from shaped hip seam to under sweetheart neckline, gathered shaping from seam over bust, padded shoulders, short inset sleeves, ground-length flared skirt patterned with wreaths of multicoloured flowers. Green and gold satin shoes, peep toes.

Sports and Leisure Wear

1 Casual wear. Brown knitted-wool sweater, high round neckline, rib matching hems of long inset sleeves, padded shoulders. Rust wool straight-cut trousers, pleats from wide waistband, side-button fastening, hip-level pockets set into side seams, wide turn-ups. Brown leather lace-up shoes. 2 Country wear. Light-green, fawn and brown wool-tweed two-piece suit: fitted hip-length single-breasted jacket, three-button fastening from waist-level to under narrow lapels, half-yoke, panel seams and shaped patch pockets with button trim, top-stitched to match edges, padded shoulders, full-length inset sleeves; knee-length box-pleated skirt. Tiny brown felt trilby-style hat. Leather gloves. Dark-green leather lace-up shoes, low wedge heels. 3 Golf. Machine-knitted yellow wool shirt, short inset sleeves, stitched cuffs, short buttoned strap fastening to under collar. Light-brown wool straight-cut trousers, pleats from waistband, side hip pockets, turn-ups, brown leather belt. Fawn felt trilby. Brown leather lace-up shoes. 4 Holiday wear. Pale-green cotton dress, semi-fitted bodice, knee-length flared skirt, self-fabric belt and covered buckle, two diagonal welt pockets over bust and hipline trimmed with green and white striped cotton to match notched collar and cuffed shirt-style sleeves, padded shoulders. White straw hat, turned-back brim. White canvas sling-back shoes, peep toes, high wedge heels. 5 Holiday wear. Cream linen dress spotted in red, pink and blue, button-through from above hemline to under collar, padded shoulders, elbow-length inset sleeves, shaped tucked shoulder yoke matches vertical hip-level pockets set above knife-pleats in knee-length flared skirt, self-fabric tie-belt. Red leather shoes, trimmed in blue, elasticated side panels, flat heels.

Accessories

1 Yellow felt spats, fur trim, leather rouleau bow fastening. 2 Tiny blue felt hat, blue silk-jersey veil. 3 Bottle-green leather handbag, threaded strap fastening, two rouleau handles. 4 Black leather handbag, clasp fastening, rouleau handles. 5 Tan leather shoes, high tongues, bow trim, high heels. 6 Pink brimless felt hat, folded crown set onto narrow band. 7 Brown felt hat, tiny crown, flat top, petersham band, wide brim, lip edge. 8 Light-brown suede lace-up shoes, perforated decoration. 9 Navy-blue leather lace-up shoes, thin platform soles, wedge heels. 10 Cream suede lace-up shoes, high heels. 11 Mustard-yellow velvet crownless hat, wide brim gathered into drawstring, self-fabric rouleau bow at back. 12 White straw hat, wide navy-blue ribbon band and bow trim on top of tiny flat crown, matching headband under turned-up brim. 13 Light-tan leather shoes, fringed tongues, metal stud trim, low thick heels. 14 Green leather shoes, tongues looped through bar straps, high wooden wedge heels. 15 Blue leather shoes, elastic inserts, thin platform soles, low wedge heels. 16 Brown leather lace-up shoes, square toes, wooden wedge heels. 17 Brimless cream felt hat, double looped crown forming bow effect. 18 Brimless evening hat, small crown covered with loops of gold organdie ribbon. 19 Ruby-red suede shoes, leather rosette trim, matching high heels. 20 Grey leather bar-strap shoes, thin platform soles, high wedge heels. 21 Black leather shoes, self-leather bow trim, high heels. 22 Navy-blue leather sling-back shoes, peep toes, high heels. 23 Brown leather clutch bag, press-stud fastening. 24 Brown leather handbag, clasp fastening, rouleau handles. 25 Natural leather handbag, flap between two handles. 26 Red leather shoes, blue trim, high heels.

1944 Day Wear

1 Silver-grey wool-crepe two-piece suit: fitted single-breasted jacket, button fastening, narrow roll collar, three-quarter-length inset sleeves, ruched shaping from short vertical seams each side centre-front, hip-length cut-away skirts; narrow knee-length skirt, unpressed pleat on centre-front. Pleated pink organdie hat, self-fabric flower trim. Black leather gloves and outsized handbag. Black and white leather shoes. 2 Turquoise wool single-breasted coat, two-button fastening, grown-on stand collar, padded shoulders, wide full-length inset sleeves, fitted bodice, side panel seams to waist-level, diagonal flap pockets set on hipline, knee-length flared skirts. Tiny bottle-green felt hat covered in grey silk-tulle, pink silk rose trim. Dark-grey leather gloves; matching clutch bag. Grey and white leather shoes. 3 Dusty-pink rayon-crepe dress, padded shoulders, tight inset sleeves, bodice and narrow knee-length skirt cut without waist seam, ruched shaping on bust and hipline from both sides of narrow central panel running from under V-shaped neckline to low hip-level. Navy-blue straw hat. Long navy-blue cotton gloves. Navy-blue and white leather shoes. 4 Three-piece dark-blue wool suit: single-breasted jacket, high two-button fastening, flap pockets, wide lapels; collarless single-breasted waistcoat; straight-cut trousers, pleats from waist, turn-ups. White cotton collar-attached shirt. Blue spotted silk tie. Dark-blue felt trilby. Black leather lace-up shoes. 5 Grey cotton dress checked in bright-green, three-button fastening, self-fabric tie-belt, wide lapels, small detachable white cotton lapels matching cuffs on short inset sleeves, padded shoulders, mock-flap pockets above bustline, knee-length flared skirt, shallow knife-pleats widely spaced at each side centre-front. Green leather shoes, peep toes.

Evening Wear

1 Double-breasted black wool tailcoat worn open, wide lapels faced in black silk. Straight-cut trousers, pleats from waist, no turn-ups. White double-breasted cotton-piqué waistcoat, low neckline, wide shawl collar. White cotton shirt worn with wing collar. White cotton-piqué bow-tie. Black fine kid-leather lace-up shoes. 2 Lilac-grey matt-silk-crepe evening dress, semi-fitted bodice, low wide sweetheart neckline, short cap sleeves gathered over padded shoulders, ruched shaping over bustline, narrow self-fabric belt, floor-length flared skirt. 3 Mustard-yellow silk-velvet dinner dress, low V-shaped neckline edged with mustard-yellow satin collar, padded shoulders, tight full-length inset sleeves, self-fabric belt and covered buckle, fitted bodice, darts under bust continued as panel seams in floor-length flared skirt, pleated shaping under bust and over hips, small posy of silk flowers worn on one shoulder. Black satin strap sandals. 4 Grey silk-chiffon evening dress, fitted bodice, ruched from centre-front seam under low shaped neckline to hip-level, narrow self-fabric rouleau shoulder straps, floor-length skirt draped over hips, gathered front panel from centre-front hipline to hem, deep-purple silk underdress. Purple kid-leather shoes, peep toes. 5 Pale-blue wool-crepe two-piece dinner suit: hip-length fitted jacket, centre-front loop and self-fabric covered button fastening from waist to under V-shaped neckline, ruched shaping from seams over bustline matching shaping from vertical seams at waist-level, padded shoulders, tight full-length inset sleeves, floor-length flared skirt. Blue velvet hair decoration; matching clutch purse. Blue leather strap sandals.

Sports and Leisure Wear

1 Holiday wear. Pink linen dress patterned with small circles of deep-blue, fastening with blue plastic triangular-shaped buttons from under collar to above knee-level, semi-fitted bodice, gathers from shoulder yoke, short cap sleeves under shoulder pads, self-fabric buttoned belt, knee-length flared skirt, pockets set into panel seams at hip-level. Blue leather lace-up shoes, low thick heels. 2 Golf. Hip-length olive-green suede top, button fastening from waist-level to under yoke seam, welt pockets on hipline, pale-green linen shirt-style collar matching long cuffed sleeves and knee-length skirt with centre-front inverted box-pleat. Dark-green leather lace-up shoes, square toes. 3 Riding. Single-breasted brown and tan wool-tweed waisted jacket, two-button fastening, wide lapels, flap pockets, flared skirts. Light-brown wool jodhpurs, turn-ups. Cream cotton collar-attached shirt. Tan wool tie. Light-brown felt hat, shallow crown, wide brim. Tan leather gloves. Tan leather elastic-sided ankle-boots. 4 Golf. Brown, fawn and rust flecked wool-tweed single-breasted jacket, three-button fastening, wide lapels, flap pockets. Fawn wool trousers, turn-ups. Light-brown wool sweater. Cream cotton collar-attached shirt. Brown wool tie. Dark-green felt trilby, shallow crown, straight brim. Brown leather lace-up shoes. 5 Riding. Mid-brown wool single-breasted jacket, three-button fastening, wide lapels, flap pockets. Yellow wool collarless single-breasted waistcoat. Dark-cream wool jodhpurs. Cream cotton collar-attached shirt. Dark-green wool tie. Light-brown felt trilby, shallow crown, brown petersham band, straight brim. Knee-high dark-brown leather boots.

Underwear and Negligee

1 Pink hip-length cotton corset, moulded and seamed cups, adjustable shoulder straps, elasticated side panels on waist and hips matching centre-front gusset above hemline, top-stitched panel seams, four adjustable suspenders, back fastening. Flesh-coloured nylon stockings. Cream leather mules, high wedge heels, feather trim. 2 Blue rayon-satin slip, self-fabric rouleau shoulder straps, low neckline edged with blue rayon lace, shaped seam above natural waist position, knee-length flared skirt. Blue satin slippers, peep toes. 3 Knee-length pale-grey wool dressing gown, wrapover front, long dark-blue roll collar edged with blue and grey twisted silk cord through to hem on front edges which matches trim on patch pockets, trim above stitched shaped cuffs of long inset sleeves and tasselled cord belt. Blue and white striped cotton pyjamas. Black leather step-in slippers. 4 Sleeveless pale-turquoise rayon-satin nightdress, pink, pale-blue and green pattern of flowers and leaves, low neckline, frill of white cotton broderie anglaise under plain rayon-satin binding, bow trim on centre-front matching hemline of ankle-length flared skirt, shaped seam above natural waistline. Turquoise satin slippers, peep toes. 5 Light-brown cotton knee-length dressing gown, dark-tan overcheck, wrapover front, plain dark-brown cotton tie-belt matching wide roll collar, welt pockets and turned-back cuffs of long inset sleeves. Brown and cream striped pyjamas. Brown leather step-in slippers.

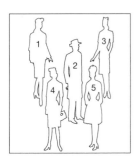

1945 Day Wear

1 Brown fake-fur hip-length unfitted jacket, single-breasted fastening with three large brown plastic buttons, wide lapels, padded shoulders, full-length inset sleeves, bound pockets set diagonally on hipline. Brown wool knee-length skirt. Brown felt brimless hat, orange silk flower trim. Light-brown leather gloves; matching clutch bag. Brown leather shoes, self-leather cross-over tabs. **2** Double-breasted camel-hair overcoat, long lapels, diagonal welt pockets on hipline, knee-length skirts. Brown wool trousers, turn-ups. White cotton collar-attached shirt. Brown silk tie matching handkerchief in breast pocket of overcoat. Dark-brown trilby. Brown leather gloves and lace-up shoes. **3** Dusty-pink wool-crepe two-piece jumper suit: hip-length collarless top, short inset sleeves, padded shoulders, top-stitched tucks under half-yoke seams above bustline matching tucks above self-fabric belt and decoration on hip-level patch pockets; knee-length flared skirt. Brown velvet ribbon-bow hair decoration. Brown leather shoes, square toes. **4** Pale-blue linen hip-length single-breasted jacket, button fastening, wide lapels, elbow-length inset sleeves, padded shoulders, two-tier frilled overskirt set wide of centre-front and under self-fabric belt and covered buckle. Navy-blue linen flared skirt. Navy-blue straw crownless hat. Navy-blue leather gloves; matching handbag. Navy-blue and white leather shoes. **5** Collarless charcoal-grey fine wool-crepe dress, front-button fastening from inset waistband to under wide lapels, full-length bishop-style inset sleeves, padded shoulders, knee-length gathered skirt, pockets set into panel seams at hip-level. Layered circles of white organdie form hat, trimmed with two large grey silk flowers. Black leather shoes trimmed with rolls of self-leather, round toes, high heels.

Evening Wear

1 Two-piece dinner suit: navy-blue hip-length top patterned with pale-blue and gold flowers, sweetheart neckline, self-fabric tailored belt and covered buckle, plain pale-blue silk elbow-length inset sleeves; matching ankle-length flared skirt, top-stitched hem, edges and detail. Gold kid strap sandals. **2** White silk-crepe evening dress patterned with bright-green flowers and leaves, low sweetheart neckline, padded shoulders, inset puff sleeves, bodice cut without waist seam from under bust seam to hem of floor-length flared skirt, panel seams each side centre-front from under bust to hem, gathered shaping under bust and over hips, self-fabric belt set into panel seams above natural waist, tied at back. **3** Cream silk-satin evening dress, low square neckline, padded shoulders, short cap sleeves, shaped tucks over bust to top seam of hip-length inset band of brown silk-satin which matches binding on hem of ground-length flared skirt and large bow hair decoration. Long brown satin gloves. **4** Black crepe cocktail dress, semi-fitted bodice ruched from V-shaped neckline to under bust and over hipline of split skirts, padded shoulders, elbow-length inset sleeves, self-fabric tailored belt and covered buckle, knee-length straight skirt. Black suede shoes. **5** Two-piece evening ensemble: hip-length pink crepe asymmetric wrapover top, waterfall frill on side hip, padded shoulders, short cap sleeves; ankle-length black crepe wrapover skirt patterned with silver and pink bows, inset self-fabric waterfall frill on side hip from waist to knee-level. Pink and white flower hair decoration. Silver kid strap sandals. **6** Black fine wool dinner dress, floor-length flared panelled skirt from high waistline, white bloused bodice, mock threaded tie with bow trim under cowl neckline, padded neckline, elbow-length inset sleeves.

Sports and Leisure Wear

1 Casual wear. Red and black flecked handknitted wool jacket, zip fastening from wide waist-level rib to under narrow ribbed stand collar which matches cuffs of long inset sleeves and four welt pockets. Dark-grey straight-cut trousers, pleats from waist, hip-level pockets set into side seams, turn-ups. Red and yellow patterned silk cravat. Black leather lace-up shoes. **2** Holiday wear. White beach dress patterned with orange and brown spots, cut-away armholes, fitted bodice, mock-wrapover front under low sweetheart neckline, self-fabric tailored belt and covered buckle, knee-length flared skirt. Green canvas sling-back shoes, peep toes, wedge heels. **3** Cycling. Cream and light-brown linen-tweed two-piece suit: single-breasted button fastening from below waist-level to under high collarless neckline, hip-length fitted bodice, padded shoulders, short inset sleeves, welt pockets over bust-level, silk handkerchief in one; knee-length flared culottes, pockets set into side seams on hipline, hand-stitched edges. Brown leather lace-up shoes, flat heels. **4** Casual wear. Olive-green linen two-piece trouser suit: edge-to-edge collarless short bolero jacket, padded shoulders, short inset sleeves, hand-stitched edges matching large hip-level patch pockets on straight-cut high-waisted trousers, self-fabric buttoned braces, turn-ups. Sleeveless yellow cotton blouse, low neckline. Dark-olive-green leather lace-up shoes, flat heels. **5** Tennis. White cotton dress, front-button fastening from above knee-length hem to under collar and revers, padded shoulders, short inset sleeves, wide split cuffs, semi-fitted bodice and flared skirt cut without waist seam, vertical pockets set into sides of decorative hip-level patches. White leather shoes, cross-straps, cut-away sides, flat heels.

Accessories

1 White leather lace-up shoes, brown leather wedge heels and platform soles. **2** Dark-red leather shoes, perforated decoration, stacked heels. **3** Navy-blue felt trilby, black ribbon trim, wide brim. **4** Brown felt trilby, high crown, straight brim. **5** Green felt trilby, wide band, turned-down brim. **6** White leather sling-back shoes, peep toes, navy-blue leather heels and platform soles. **7** Cream leather shoes, peep toes, wedge heels. **8** Red leather sling-back shoes, peep toes, platform soles. **9** Light-grey felt trilby, high crown, navy-blue ribbon trim. **10** Brown leather lace-up shoes, stacked heels. **11** Olive-green leather bar-strap shoes, high heels. **12** Cream leather shoes, ankle straps, buckle fastening, cut-away sides, black leather toecaps and high heels. **13** Black leather lace-up shoes. **14** Brimless hat covered with tiny silk flowers, satin bow trim. **15** Green suede elastic-sided shoes, wedge heels, thin platform soles. **16** Brown felt hat, trim of two orange feathers. **17** Brown leather lace-up shoes, perforated decoration, stacked heels. **18** Green felt hat, tiny crown, flat top, red ribbon-and-bow trim matching edge of brim. **19** Navy-blue felt hat, high crown, flat top, self-felt band-and-bow trim over wide peak. **20** Draped grey silk-jersey brimless hat. **21** Tan leather sling-back shoes, bar straps, platform soles, stud trim, high heels. **22** Dark-grey suede shoes, leather heels. **23** Draped black wool turban with top-knot. **24** Brimless fawn wool-tweed hat, draped through loop on centre-front. **25** Bottle-green felt hat, tiny crown, flat top, turned-up brim, fringed edge. **26** Brown leather lace-up shoes, top-stitched detail, high heels. **27** White straw hat, tall crown, flat top, wide split red silk ribbon matching edge of wide brim. **28** Tan leather shoes, self-leather curled tongues, top-stitched detail, high heels.

1946 Day Wear

1 Bottle-green wool dress, fitted bodice, three-quarter-length inset sleeves, padded shoulders, knee-length gathered skirt, hip-level welt pockets, self-fabric covered button trim, shoulder-wide white cotton-piqué bertha collar, hand-stitched edges. Black leather shoes, high heels. 2 Pale-grey wool double-breasted coat, wide lapels, bracelet-length inset sleeves, padded shoulders, front panels of bodice and skirts cut without waist seam, upper side panel seamed above waist-level, lower side panel seamed on hipline, vertical pockets set into seams at hip-level. Red silk scarf. Red wool beret with stalk. Grey leather gloves; matching sling-back shoes, high heels.
3 Cream, pale-green and apricot flecked linen-tweed dress, fitted bodice from top-stitched hip seam which matches finish on high round neckline, short inset sleeves, padded shoulders, narrow knee-length skirt. Bottle-green linen turban. Beige leather gloves; matching shoes, peep toes. 4 Grey wool double-breasted knee-length overcoat, wide lapels, large collar, inset sleeves, buttoned strap at wrist-level, self-fabric belt, leather buckle, large patch-and-flap pockets, top-stitched edges and detail. Dark-grey wool trousers, turn-ups. Navy-blue and red spotted silk scarf. Dark-blue felt trilby. Black leather gloves and shoes. 5 Two-piece cherry-red wool suit: collarless single-breasted long jacket, button fastening from hip-level to under high neckline, three-quarter-length inset sleeves, black buckled leather belt; narrow knee-length skirt. Small black straw hat trimmed with red, black and grey silk flowers. Black leather gloves; matching large handbag and plain high-heeled shoes.

Wedding Wear

1 Frost-white silk-crepe wedding dress, bloused bodice above narrow self-fabric belt, top-stitched scalloped yoke matching finish of high round neckline, long fitted inset sleeves, long point over hand, padded shoulders, ground-length flared skirt with train. Headdress of wax flowers, long silk-tulle veil. 2 White silk-taffeta wedding dress, fitted bodice, V-shaped point on front, off-the-shoulder cape collar under high round neckline, long fitted inset sleeves, point over hand, padded shoulders, ground-length gathered skirt. Earphone headdress of real flowers, matching small bouquet, two-tier silk-tulle veil. 3 Ivory-white crepe wedding dress, low V-shaped neckline, long fitted sleeves, padded shoulders, upper bodice draped from seam under bust, lower bodice draped and swathed from central knot to hip-level, ground-length flared skirt. Long ivory-white silk-tulle veil from silk flower headdress.
4 Cream crepe wedding dress, fitted bodice, V-shaped point on centre-front, high neckline split to rounded yoke seam, gathered shaping under seam, long fitted inset sleeves, point over hand, padded shoulders, ground-length flared skirt, panel of unpressed pleats at front, long train. Headdress of silk lilies, long silk-tulle veil. 5 Cream silk-taffeta wedding dress, fitted bodice from hipline seam, low square neckline with rounded edges, long fitted inset sleeves, self-fabric covered buttons above wrists, padded shoulders, ground-length flared skirt, gathered side panels, short train. Headdress of silk flowers, long silk-tulle veil.

Sports and Leisure Wear

1 Holiday wear. One-piece cream linen beach suit patterned in red: fitted bra top, wide shoulder straps, triangular bib, point on centre of low neckline and attached to wide waist of tailored shorts, flared legs with turn-ups, hand-stitched edges and detail.
2 Cycling. Apricot handknitted wool sweater, sunray pattern from under wide banded high round neckline, short inset sleeves, padded shoulders. Brown wool above-knee-length flared culottes, wide waistband, double row of buttons above wide box-pleats each side centre-front. Brown leather lace-up shoes, low wedge heels, thin platform soles. 3 Tennis. White cotton blouse, buttoned-strap fastening, narrow lapels, long pointed collar, shaped yoke seam, short inset sleeves, stitched cuffs. Above-knee-length flared white linen culottes, grown-on waistband, four-button fastening above central creases, hip-level welt pockets. White leather lace-up shoes, flat heels. 4 Golf/casual wear. Hip-length petrol-blue wool jacket, zip fastening from above self-fabric buttoned belt to under wide lapels, decorative panel seams curve over bust and hipline, pockets set into seams at hip-level, full-length inset sleeves gathered into cuffs, top-stitched edges and detail. Straight-cut dark-grey wool-flannel trousers with turn-ups. Draped green wool-jersey turban. Black leather shoes, strap-and-buckle fastening, flat heels. 5 Golf. Single-breasted black, brown and rust checked wool-tweed jacket, wide lapels, shoulder yoke, self-fabric belt, leather buckle, large hip-level patch pockets, side openings. Straight-cut brown wool-flannel trousers with turn-ups. White cotton collar-attached shirt. Rust-brown wool tie. Dark-brown felt trilby, wide brim turned up on one side. Brown and cream leather lace-up shoes, toecaps, stacked heels.

Underwear and Negligee

1 Peach cotton-satin bra covered in self-colour cotton lace, seamed cups, narrow ribbon adjustable shoulder straps, back fastening. Cream cotton hip girdle patterned with peach satin flowers, top-stitched seamed control panels, elasticated front gussets and side panels, four elasticated suspenders. Flesh-coloured nylon stockings.
2 All-in-one pink cotton bra and girdle, raised self-colour lace pattern, seamed cups, adjustable shoulder straps, top-stitched control panels, elasticated front gusset and side panels, top-stitched edges, lace trim, four adjustable ribbon suspenders. Flesh-coloured nylon stockings. Pink velvet mules, satin ribbon trim, high heels. 3 Pale-blue silk ankle-length nightdress, shaped seam above waist-level, low V-shaped neckline, coffee lace trim and border. Matching short bolero, high round neckline, self-fabric bow tie, short inset puff sleeves. Pale-blue quilted satin slippers, feather trim.
4 Pale-green silk camiknickers patterned with self-colour satin spots, low neckline, shaping above curved half seam under bust, side panel seams, centre-front seam, flared legs, top-stitched hems, self-fabric rouleau shoulder straps. 5 Lilac-grey silk-jersey housecoat, zip fastening from shaped waist seam through ruched inset cummerbund to under low V-shaped neckline, draped shaping from padded shoulders to under bust seam, long sleeves gathered into armholes and into ruched cuffs, ground-length bias-cut skirts.

1947 Day Wear

1 Silver-grey wool dress, fitted bodice, high round neckline, centre split to bust-level, three-quarter-length inset sleeves, no shoulder pads, self-fabric belt and covered buckle, hip yoke, mid-calf-length straight skirt, gathered front panel. Charcoal-grey felt beret. Black leather gloves; matching shoes, ankle straps, high heels. 2 Crimson wool jumper suit: fitted bodice, long dolman sleeves, white cotton cuffs matching collar, tucked shoulder yoke with centre-front notch, self-fabric belt and covered buckle, narrow hip basque worn over small pads; mid-calf-length panelled skirt. Dark-brown felt hat, padded brim. Dark-brown leather shoes, peep toes. 3 Petrol-blue wool coat, double-breasted fastening from waist to under wide lapels, high collar, long inset sleeves, rounded shoulderline, no pads, set of two welt pockets on hipline, button trim, full mid-calf-length skirts, small bust and hip pads. Black felt hat, bright-green and blue feather trim. Black gloves. Black leather shoes, shaped sides, high heels. 4 Black and grey flecked wool-tweed two-piece suit: hip-length single-breasted fitted jacket, narrow lapels, small collar, long inset sleeves, rounded shoulderline, no pads, angled welt pockets, button trim; straight mid-calf-length skirt, single knife-pleat on centre-front. Brimless black straw hat, silk flower trim. Black leather gloves. Grey umbrella, long black handle. Black leather shoes. 5 Dark-mustard-yellow taffeta dress, fitted bodice, self-fabric covered button fastening from low hip seam to under small stand collar, long inset sleeves, rounded shoulderline, no pads, mid-calf-length skirt gathered from shaped hip seam, small hip and bust pads. Lacquered black straw hat, tiny crown, wide brim turned down. Black leather shoes, ankle straps, cut-away sides, peep toes, high heels.

Evening Wear

1 Black silk-taffeta evening dress, fitted bodice, small waist, low neckline, narrow self-fabric rouleau shoulder straps, decorative off-the-shoulder frilled cape, ground-length flared skirt from low hip seam, set of unpressed pleats on side. 2 Black silk-chiffon evening dress, fitted bodice draped from small waist to under bust, strapless upper bodice, draped stole over one shoulder trimmed with two outsized pink silk peonies, ground-length pleated skirt, black silk under-bodice and underskirt follow the same shape. Long black silk gloves. 3 Ice-blue silk-taffeta evening dress, fitted boned strapless bodice, low neckline decorated with dark-blue, pink and crystal beads matching hem of ice-blue silk-chiffon overskirt, ground-length taffeta underskirt, both skirts gathered from waist. Long ice-blue satin gloves. 4 Dusty-pink silk-satin evening dress, fitted bodice, low neckline banded in self-fabric to match wide shoulder and off-the-shoulder straps, infilled with pale-coffee lace matching bra-shaped upper bodice and narrow frilled cape, ground-length flared panelled skirt. 5 Taffeta dinner dress, fitted shirt-style bodice in black, button fastening from above self-fabric belt and covered buckle, pointed collar worn turned up at back of neck, short inset sleeves, split cuffs, coral-pink skirt, mid-calf-length at front, dipping to ground at back, pleated black lace overskirt following same shape. Black satin gloves; matching strap sandals, ankle straps, open sides, high heels.

Sports and Leisure Wear

1 Golf. Collarless handknitted cardigan, brown V-shaped front panel incorporating narrow shoulder yoke matching full-length inset sleeves, ribbed cuffs, main body in light-fawn, button fastening from deep rib to under high round neckline. Below-knee-length flared skirt checked in autumn colours, large single patch pocket on side of left hip. Brown wool peaked cap. Brown leather lace-up shoes. 2 Golf. Dark-green waterproofed-cotton two-piece suit: short bloused jacket, zip fastening from wide waistband to under knitted collar, shoulder yoke, large patch-and-flap pockets, long inset sleeves, buttoned cuffs, top-stitched edges and detail; straight-cut trousers, pleated from waist, turn-ups. Peaked cap in matching fabric. Brown leather step-in shoes. 3 Country wear. Beige wool-tweed edge-to-edge sleeveless jacket, single loop-and-button fastening under small collar, held at waist by wide brown leather buckled belt, large patch pockets attached to hems of hip-length rounded skirts. Sage-green wool dress, shirt-style sleeves, below-knee-length flared skirt, central inverted box-pleat, side button fastening. Brown felt brimless hat. Brown leather lace-up shoes, thick heels. 4 Casual wear. Straight-cut rust wool trousers and sideless top, long keyhole opening under small collar, pleats from under inset waistband, no turn-ups. Light-brown wool handknitted sweater, long inset sleeves, deep ribbed hems. Cream, rust and green patterned silk scarf. Brown leather lace-up shoes. 5 Tennis. White cotton blouse and skirt: unfitted top, low square neckline, wide self-fabric binding matching edges of cap sleeves; short flared skirt, large box-pleat at front under buttoned waistband. White cotton peaked cap. White cotton ankle socks. White canvas lace-up shoes.

Accessories

1 Navy-blue leather shoes, rolled tongue trim. 2 Crownless pink straw hat, wide brim, two large hat pins. 3 Grey felt hat, black feather trim. 4 Black leather handbag, two rouleau handles. 5 Beige leather shoes, top-stitched detail, platform soles, high heels. 6 Red leather sling-back shoes, openwork detail, peep toes. 7 Beige felt hat, self-colour satin bow trim matching binding on wide brim. 8 Bottle-green leather handbag, wooden handle. 9 Navy-blue leather handbag, flap with decorative clasp fastening, top-stitched edges, long rouleau handles. 10 Black suede shoes, ankle straps, open sides, peep toes, platform soles, high heels. 11 Brown leather shoes, high tongues, strap-and-buckle trim, square toes, low heels. 12 Gold kid strap sandals, high heels. 13 Mustard-yellow felt hat, trimmed with green velvet leaves and yellow berries. 14 Brimless maroon felt hat, self-fabric bow trim on back. 15 Red leather shoes, high pointed tongues matching backs, rouleau bow trim, thin platform soles, high wedge heels. 16 Black satin strap sandals, medium heels. 17 Navy-blue felt hat, wide navy-blue and white striped silk ribbon trim matching binding on edge of wide turned-up brim. 18 Brimless red straw hat, black pom-pon trim on top. 19 Tan leather bag, flap-and-clasp fastening, long handle. 20 Olive-green leather shoes, high tongues, self-leather bow trim, top-stitched edges. 21 Tan canvas shoulderbag, flap with leather strap-and-stud fastening matching long handle. 22 Pale-grey leather shoes, top-stitched navy-blue leather strap trim, keyhole opening under rouleau bow, peep toes, wedge heels. 23 Wine-red brimless felt hat, feather pom-pon trim. 24 Crocodile handbag, clasp fastening. 25 Crocodile sling-back shoes, high tongues, draped trim, high heels.

1948 Day Wear

1 Dull-grey silk dress, three-quarter-length dolman sleeves cut in one with fitted bodice, high neckline slashed and rounded off at front, narrow self-fabric belt and covered buckle, mid-calf-length flared skirt, deep tuck over padded hips. Brimless black felt hat, domed crown, self-felt trim on one side. Long black leather gloves. Plain black leather shoes, high heels. Black silk rolled umbrella, long handle. 2 Lilac and grey striped wool dress, fitted bodice, shaped yoke trimmed with three buttons to match trim above white cotton cuffs of long inset sleeves and large hip-level patch pockets, narrow self-fabric belt and covered buckle, mid-calf-length accordion-pleated skirt. Plain black leather shoes. 3 Deep-blue wool edge-to-edge hip-length flared jacket, wide three-quarter-length dolman sleeves, deep turned-back cuffs, small stand collar. Mid-calf-length straight-cut black wool skirt. Brimless black felt hat, deep-blue feather pom-pon trim. Long black leather gloves. Plain black leather shoes, high heels. 4 Rust-brown linen dress, short dolman sleeves, fitted bodice, asymmetric fastening under small collar, leather buttons, diagonal seaming over bustline matching hip-level detail, pocket concealed in upper seam, self-fabric belt and covered buckle, mid-calf-length flared skirt. Plain brown leather shoes, high heels. 5 Double-breasted navy-blue wool jacket, long wide lapels, patch pockets, silk handkerchief in breast pocket. Light-grey flannel straight-cut trousers, turn-ups. White cotton collar-attached shirt. Blue and grey striped silk tie. Grey felt trilby, narrow self-colour ribbon band, wide brim worn turned up at back. Black leather lace-up shoes, no toecaps.

Evening Wear

1 Black silk-taffeta evening dress, wide boat-shaped neckline, fitted bodice from hip-level to under bust, upper bodice with gathered shaping under bust, black shiny sequin trim matching three-quarter-length inset sleeves and two wide bands set into ground-length gathered skirt. 2 Ice-blue satin evening dress, delicately patterned with pin-head spots of black and gold, fitted bodice between off-the-shoulder band of ruched self-fabric and matching band on hipline, ground-length gathered skirt from hip-level. Silver kid strap sandals. 3 Formal dinner dress, white silk-chiffon upper bodice, gathered shaping from seam under bust, low V-shaped off-the-shoulder neckline, three-quarter-length sleeves gathered from shoulder and into narrow cuffs, fitted lower bodice of white silk-taffeta patterned with pale-blue, silver and pink flowers matching ground-length flared skirt. 4 Navy-blue satin evening dress, fitted boned strapless bodice, low shaped neckline edged with bias-cut 'collar' in silver satin with navy-blue velvet spot pattern, ground-length skirt gathered from V-pointed waist seam. Navy-blue satin shoes. 5 Pale-silver-grey silk-taffeta evening gown, fitted ruched bodice, wide off-the-shoulder collar ruched to one side, tightly-fitted elbow-length sleeves, ground-length flared skirt, centre-front unpressed inverted box-pleat. Silver kid shoes, peep toes.

Sports and Leisure Wear

1 Tennis. Short white linen dress, semi-fitted bodice above inset waistband, button fastening from under long pointed collar to hip-level above two box-pleats, short dolman sleeves and yoke cut in one piece, triangular-shaped mock-flap pockets set into yoke seam matching flaps on hip-level patch pockets, piped pockets above with button trim. White cotton ankle socks. White canvas lace-up sports shoes. 2 Leisure wear. Green and yellow striped cotton sleeveless playsuit, square neckline, gathered shaping from under yoke seam to inset waistband, button fastening from under deep armhole to hip-level on one side, wide stitched turn-ups. Yellow cotton blouse, pointed collar, short dolman sleeves, stitched cuffs. Leather sandals. 3 Country wear. Short flared edge-to-edge brown and tan flecked wool-tweed coat, wide three-quarter-length dolman sleeves, deep turned-back cuffs, long shawl collar, large hip-level patch-and-flap pockets. Brown wool sweater; matching skirt. Brimless brown felt hat, self-felt bow trim. Brown leather gloves and shoes. 4 Tennis. White cotton collar-attached shirt, buttoned-strap opening, short inset sleeves, stitched cuffs, single breast patch pocket. Tailored white linen shorts, deep waistband, side hip pockets, no turn-ups. White cotton socks. White canvas lace-up shoes. 5 Holiday wear. White cotton dress patterned with blue and orange irregular spots, front button fastening from above hemline of narrow mid-calf-length skirt to under high neckline, short cap sleeves, fitted bodice, narrow self-fabric belt and covered buckle, bias-cut waterfall frill bound in blue cotton falling from waist-level to above hemline under button fastening. Dark-blue nylon-gauze hat, shallow crown, wide turned-down brim. Blue leather handbag; matching shoes, peep toes.

Underwear and Negligee

1 White silk all-in-one pyjama suit, green, pink and blue flower pattern, fitted lower bodice from waist to under bust, sleeveless upper bodice, gathered shaping under bust, low V-shaped wrapover neckline, ankle-length wide flared trousers. Green satin slippers, flat heels. 2 Pink cotton bra, seamed cups, self-colour lace trim, narrow ribbon shoulder straps, back fastening. Pink cotton front-fastening corset, stitched panel seams, elasticated side panels, four adjustable suspenders. Flesh-coloured nylon stockings. 3 White cotton corset incorporating bra, seamed cups, appliqué lace trim matching front panel of corset, elasticated cotton side panels, narrow ribbon shoulder straps, four adjustable suspenders. Flesh-coloured nylon stockings. 4 White cotton housecoat spotted in pale-blue, fitted bodice, V-shaped neckline and edge of zip fastening trimmed with self-fabric frill to match cuffs of shirt-style sleeves, ground-length skirt gathered from shaped hip yoke. 5 Quilted cream silk-satin dressing gown, multicoloured pattern of flowers, wrapover front fastening on one side with plain cream silk ribbon bow which matches wide lapels, small collar and bound hems of full-length flared sleeves, knee-length flared panelled skirts. Collarless cream satin pyjamas, self-fabric covered buttons, wide flared trousers. Cream satin slippers, multicoloured silk pom-pon trim. 6 Red wool double-breasted housecoat, black buttons, large shoulder-wide cape collar, black wool edging matching front edge, shaped cuffs on long inset sleeves and hip-level patch pockets, ground-length flared skirts.

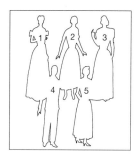

1949 Day Wear

1 Light-brown waterproofed-cotton raincoat, single-breasted fastening, wide lapels, large collar worn turned up, raglan sleeves, self-fabric belt, leather buckle, diagonal hip-level welt pockets, top-stitched edges and detail. Brown wool trousers with turn-ups. Blue and white striped cotton collar-attached shirt. Blue and brown spotted silk tie. Brown trilby. Brown leather gloves and lace-up shoes. **2** Light-grey/blue wool-tweed double-breasted unfitted coat flecked in navy-blue, large buttons, wide lapels, large collar, raglan sleeves, split turned-back cuffs, hip-level welt pockets, top-stitched edges and detail. Navy-blue felt hat, wide ribbon band, narrow brim, fine veil. Navy-blue leather shoes. **3** Yellow and grey flecked linen-tweed dress, button fastening from above hemline of flared panelled skirt to under narrow shawl collar, fitted bodice, shaped seam under bust, gathered shaping, elbow-length dolman sleeves, self-fabric belt and covered buckle. Dark-grey suede shoes, peep toes, high heels. **4** Two-piece grey wool suit: single-breasted fitted jacket, flared skirts over padded hips, self-fabric belt and covered buckle, half-yoke seam above bust-level, inset cuffs of silver-grey silk with fine black spots matching lapels, collar and turned-back cuffs of three-quarter-length dolman sleeves; mid-calf-length straight skirt. Brimless black felt hat, grey and black feather trim. Black leather gloves; matching shoes. **5** Dark-red wool single-breasted coat, fitted bodice and full skirts cut in flared panels without waist seam, button fastening from padded hipline to under wide rounded lapels, top-stitched edges, full-length inset sleeves from dropped shoulderline. Mid-grey felt hat, narrow turned-back brim, self-felt trim. Light-grey silk scarf. Grey gloves. Black leather handbag; matching shoes.

Evening Wear

1 Turquoise and silver silk-brocade evening dress, fitted boned strapless bodice, ground-length flared skirt, unpressed knife-pleats each side centre-front, low neckline trimmed with tucked cuff of plain deep-turquoise silk-satin matching wide cummerbund and large bow trim on off-the-shoulder strap. Above-elbow-length deep-turquoise satin gloves. **2** Silver-grey satin evening dress, fitted boned strapless bodice, self-fabric overbodice split to waist on centre-front, ankle-length skirt gathered from waist. Silver kid shoes, wrapover detail, peep toes. **3** Dark-green and black printed silk-taffeta evening dress, draped fitted bodice incorporating wide off-the-shoulder cape collar to elbow-level, ground-length flared skirt worn over petticoats. Elbow-length black satin gloves; matching shoes. **4** Two-piece black wool evening suit: double-breasted jacket, wide lapels faced with black satin matching button fastening and trim on inset sleeves, piped pockets; straight-cut trousers, no turn-ups. White silk collar-attached shirt. Black satin bow-tie. Black patent-leather lace-up shoes. **5** Burgundy-red silk evening dress, sleeveless fitted bodice, low sweetheart neckline, ruched shaping over bust, horizontal tucks above waist seam, gold embroidery and bead trim on wide shoulder straps, ankle-length flared skirt. Above-elbow-length black satin gloves; matching plain shoes, medium-high heels.

Sports and Leisure Wear

1 Ski wear. Dark-green weatherproof cotton jacket, zip fastening from above hem of hip-length skirts to under pointed collar, raglan sleeves, buttoned cuffs, hip-level welt pockets, chest-level zipped pockets, inset waistband with button-and-strap adjustment at side. Black weatherproof cotton trousers gathered at ankle-level and tucked into black leather ski-boots. Black wool neck-scarf. Green cotton peaked cap. **2** Ski wear. Blue weatherproof corded-cotton jacket, zip fastening from above hems of hip-level skirts to under chin of hood, drawstring fastening matching waist, shaping from under yoke seam, long inset sleeves gathered into cuffs, large hip-level patch-and-flap pockets. Dark-blue weatherproof cotton trousers, gathered at ankle-level and worn tucked into black leather ski-boots. Red leather mittens. **3** Holiday wear. Pale-blue cotton dress, all-over pattern of yellow spots, button fastening from hip-level to under narrow shawl collar, short semi-raglan sleeves, turned-back cuffs, self-fabric belt and covered buckle, hip-level patch pockets, flared skirt. Dark-blue leather strap sandals. **4** Winter sports wear. Bottle-green corded-wool waist-length jacket, double-breasted fastening, matching waistband, wide lapels, full-length raglan sleeves gathered into cuffs. Black wool trousers, pleats from waist, legs narrow to hems, stirrups under feet. Orange wool neck-scarf; matching brimless hat, black pom-pon trim. Large sunglasses. Black leather ski-boots. **5** Holiday wear. Red and white patterned cotton two-piece beach suit: strapless bra top, neckline cuffed in plain navy-blue cotton knotted on centre-front; matching buttoned waistband of short skirt, narrow knife-pleats from hip yoke.

Accessories

1 Black straw hat, pink rose trim. **2** Brown leather shoes, high tongues, strap-and-buckle trim, thick heels. **3** Brimless grey felt hat, self-felt flower trim. **4** Navy-blue straw hat, wide brim, cut detail. **5** Cream quilted leather shoes. **6** Brown leather handbag, rouleau handles, brass trim. **7** Red nylon umbrella, long red plastic handle. **8** Black silk evening bag, pearl bead trim. **9** Grey leather handbag, wide strap handle. **10** Grey suede shoes, perforated leaf design. **11** Green leather handbag, rouleau handles, brass clasp and trim. **12** Brown leather ankle-boots, laces, high heels. **13** Pink wool-jersey hat, rouleau trim. **14** Navy-blue leather bag, brass clasp and trim. **15** Red leather shoes, bow trim, flat heels. **16** Brown silk evening bag, long handle, gold clasp. **17** White nylon gloves, pleated cuffs. **18** Grey suede gloves, scalloped cuffs. **19** Black satin gloves, embroidered-flower trim. **20** Brown leather golf shoes, fringed tongues. **21** Brown leather sandals, strap-and-buckle fastening, crepe soles. **22** Yellow leather pumps, blue lacing and ankle straps. **23** Green leather strap sandals. **24** Brimless straw hat, uneven edge, top-stitching. **25** Black satin evening bag, bead trim. **26** Tan leather lace-up shoes, stitched trim. **27** Black suede shoes, open sides, cross straps, peep toes, thick heels. **28** Black satin T-strap shoes, nylon-mesh strap fronts, high heels. **29** Beige leather drum-shaped handbag, thick handle, brass fittings. **30** Black satin shoes, open sides, rouleau strap trim, high heels. **31** Grey suede sling-back shoes, high wedge heels, top-stitched strap straps. **32** Brimless yellow wool beret. **33** Cream leather sling-back shoes, peep toes, high heels, platform soles. **34** Brown leather bag, wide strap handle, top-stitched detail, brass trim. **35** Black leather step-in shoes.

Chart of the Development of 1940s Fashion
Biographies of Designers
Sources for 1940s Fashion

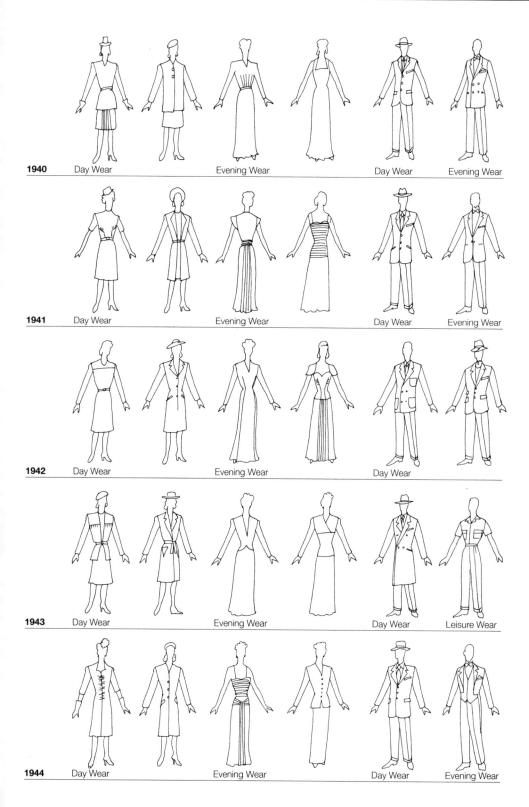

1940 Day Wear — Evening Wear — Day Wear — Evening Wear

1941 Day Wear — Evening Wear — Day Wear — Evening Wear

1942 Day Wear — Evening Wear — Day Wear

1943 Day Wear — Evening Wear — Day Wear — Leisure Wear

1944 Day Wear — Evening Wear — Day Wear — Evening Wear

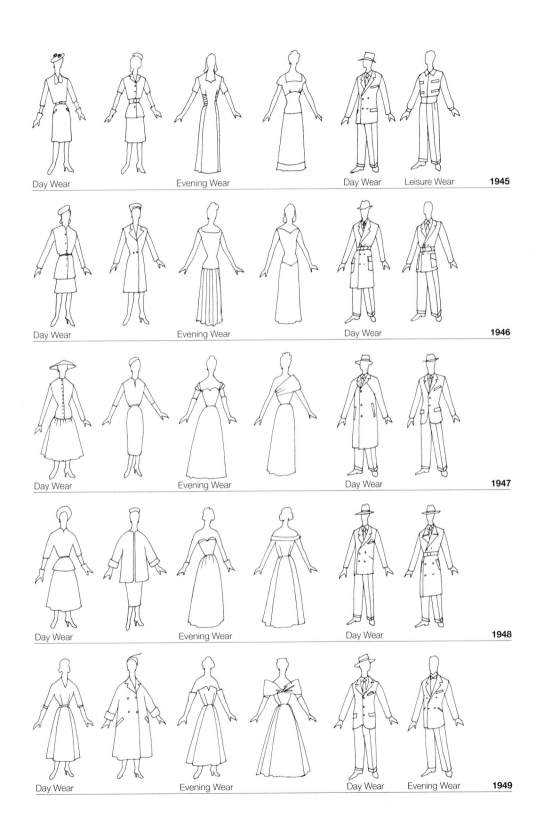

Day Wear   Evening Wear   Day Wear   Leisure Wear   **1945**

Day Wear   Evening Wear   Day Wear   **1946**

Day Wear   Evening Wear   Day Wear   **1947**

Day Wear   Evening Wear   Day Wear   **1948**

Day Wear   Evening Wear   Day Wear   Evening Wear   **1949**

Adrian (Adrian Adolph Greenburg) 1903–59. Costume designer. Born Naugatuck, Connecticut, USA. In the 1930s Adrian was Hollywood's most influential designer. His many widely copied designs include a slouch hat worn by Greta Garbo in *A Woman of Affairs* (1929) and a white organdie dress with ruffled sleeves for Joan Crawford in *Letty Lynton* (1932). Several 1930s designs, such as his pillbox hat for Garbo in *As You Desire Me* (1932) and Hedy Lamarr's snood in *I Take This Woman*, were precursors to 1940s trends. As well as his work for the cinema, he also created chic, wearable suits, sometimes decorated with appliqué. Following his retirement in 1942, Adrian opened a boutique in Beverly Hills, California.

Amies, (Sir) Hardy (Erwin) 1909–. Designer. Born London, England. Amies started his career in fashion at Lachasse in 1934. In 1945 he opened his own couture house and became known for refined, well-cut women's suits in tweed and wool and for sumptuous puff-sleeved ball gowns. He continued to be hugely successful into the following decade, receiving the Royal Warrant to design clothes for the Queen in 1955. In 1961 he began designing menswear.

Balenciaga, Cristobal 1895–1972. Designer. Born Guetaria, Spain. At the age of 20 Balenciaga opened his first house in San Sebastian. When he moved to Paris in 1937 he was already Spain's leading couturier, producing austere, elegant, well-cut clothes in sombre colours recognizable for their stark Spanish style. In 1939 his tight-waisted dresses with dropped shoulderlines were clear forerunners of Dior's New Look of 1947. During the 1940s Balenciaga's reputation for highly influential, dramatic designs grew. Nineteen forty-six saw the launch of his 'barrel line' as well as embroidered boleros based on toreador's costumes. His many innovations include the pillbox hat, first shown in the mid-1940s, the stand-away collar, and the sack dress of 1956.

Balmain, Pierre (Alexandre) 1914–82. Designer. Born St Jean de Maurienne, France. Balmain started his career with Molyneux. In 1941 he began working at Lelong where he met Dior.

Balmain set up his own couture house in 1945 and found instant success with his bell-shaped skirts with nipped-in waists similar to those later produced by Dior for the New Look. Though he tended to favour a narrow silhouette for his suits and dresses, Balmain was also known for his full half-belted coats and romantic full-skirted ball gowns. During the 1950s he created his famous sheath dresses, worn under jackets, as well as stoles for day wear and cossack-style wraps.

Carnegie, Hattie (Henrietta Kanengeiser) 1889–1956. Designer, manufacturer. Born Vienna, Austria. Carnegie began her career at the age of 15 at Macy's department store, New York, dressing hats. She moved into clothing design in 1913 and launched her first collection in 1918. Her first ready-to-wear collection followed in 1928. Carnegie was best known for grey tailored suits and black dresses which she sold in her own retail stores across America. Her success was largely due to an ability to adapt Paris haute-couture fashion to the US market, where her chic, conservative clothes became highly sought after.

Creed, Charles 1909–66. Designer. Born Paris, France. Creed studied tailoring and art in Vienna, then worked for Linton Tweeds in Carlisle and the department store Bergdorf Goodman in New York. He joined his family's tailoring firm in Paris in the 1930s. The house closed during World War II, though Creed continued to design while on leave from the army and contributed to the Utility Scheme. He opened his own house after the war, establishing a reputation for refined, precisely cut suits in wool and tweed. During the late 1940s he also collaborated with a number of US sportswear manufacturers.

Dessès, Jean (Jean Dimitre Verginie) 1904–70. Designer. Born Alexandria, Egypt, of Greek parents. Dessès began his career at the age of 21 with Maison Jane. He opened his own house in 1937 and launched his first ready-to-wear line, 'Jean Dessès Diffusion', in 1949. During the 1940s he was known for his draped evening dresses inspired by ancient Greek and Egyptian garments, and for his

embroidered ball gowns and sheath dresses worn with close-fitting jackets.

Dior, Christian 1905–57. Designer. Born Granville, France. Dior began his fashion career in Paris at the age of 30, selling fashion sketches to newspapers. He joined Robert Piguet in 1938 and worked briefly for Lelong in 1942 before opening his own house in 1946. In 1947 his first collection, the 'Corolle line', soon nicknamed the 'New Look', was sensationally successful. His curved bodices and huge skirts with nipped-in waists brought a new femininity and glamour to fashion after the severe broad-shouldered, narrow-skirted lines produced under wartime rationing. While some were shocked by the enormous quantities of cloth required for such an exaggerated silhouette, most women followed the style and the 'Corolle line' remains the most famous single collection ever presented. In his 1948 and 1949 collections Dior developed the New Look shape, adding flounced sleeves or bulk at chest-level above a tightly belted waist. He also included jackets featuring *trompe l'oeil* details and full skirts with uneven hemlines. During the 1950s Dior continued to create highly influential and increasingly sophisticated designs such as three-piece outfits of cardigan, top and skirt, the princess line, coolie hats, horseshoe collars and his own versions of the caftan and cheongsam.

Fath, Jacques 1912–54. Designer. Born Maison-Lafitte, France. During the 1930s Fath worked as a stockbroker at the Paris Bourse while at the same time studying costume and fashion design. He opened his own house in 1937, achieving worldwide fame by the late 1940s. Fath attracted a young, sophisticated clientele with his extravagant, flirtatious evening dresses and jaunty day clothes, often with decorative pleats, darts and angled collars.

Grès Couture house. Founded in 1941 by Paris-born Germaine Krebs (1903–93). Krebs had trained with Premet and in 1934 she opened a couture house, 'Alix', in association with Julie Barton. 'Alix' closed in 1939. 'Madame Grès', as Krebs became known at her own house, was famous for draped and pleated dresses – in silk and

wool – which resemble classical Greek robes, often cut on the bias and with dolman sleeves. She adopted a sculptural approach to dressmaking, each garment being modelled on the mannequin by hand with minimal use of patterns or cutting.

Hartnell, (Sir) Norman 1901–79. Designer. Born London, England. Hartnell worked at Madame Désirée, Esther's and with Lucile before opening his own premises in London in 1923. His career took off during the late 1920s when he became famous for his extravagant wedding dresses, though he also designed for the theatre and for films. He was appointed dressmaker to the British Royal Family in 1938 and created Elizabeth II's wedding dress and coronation gown as well as designing many outfits for her overseas tours. His designs were central in forming the image of the royal family. He also became known for fine tailoring and for his use of woollen tweed in suits and coats. In the 1940s Hartnell went on to produce his own ready-to-wear lines.

Jacques Heim 1899–1967. Designer. Born Paris, France. Heim designed womenswear for his parent's fur business until the 1930s, when he founded his own couture house. His company closed during World War II. In 1946 he opened a chain of sportswear boutiques and became famous for his 'Atome' two-piece bathing suit of 1950 – the first bikini. He was the first couturier to use cotton for beachwear. During the 1950s he was also known for his halter-neck tops worn with knee-length madras shorts.

James, Charles (William Brega) 1906–78. Designer. Born Sandhurst, England. James began his fashion career when he opened a hat shop in Chicago in 1924 under the name 'Charles Bouchéron'. He created his first dress collection in New York in 1928, his first London collection in 1929, and his first Paris collection in 1934. By 1940 he had returned to New York and established a house under his own name where he based his operation for most of the 1940s and 1950s. An architect of dress, James created superbly cut, sculpted ball gowns using large quantities of lavish fabrics often arranged asymmetrically in bunches and folds. He was also well known for his highly structured coats, his dresses with spiral zips and his quilted ivory-satin jackets.

Lelong, Lucien 1889–1958. Designer. Born Paris, France. Lelong trained at the Hautes Etudes des Commerciales, Paris, and established his own business after World War I. He became known for his skilful use of beautiful fabrics in creating elegant, understated dresses and eveningwear. Lelong was one of the first designers to produce stockings and lingerie and in the late 1930s he designed tight-waisted, full skirts which were precursors to Dior's 'New Look' of 1947. During World War II Lelong was president of the Chambre Syndicale de la Haute Couture and was instrumental in persuading the occupying German forces not to move Parisian couture houses to Berlin. His last collection in 1947 included narrow dresses, pleated harem hemlines and broad-shouldered suits with cutaway fronts and nipped-in waists.

Mainbocher (Main Rousseau Bocher) 1891–1976. Designer. Born Chicago, USA. Mainbocher was the first American couturier to achieve success in Paris, opening his own house there in 1930. He became famous for embroidered, apron-style evening dresses, for his use of the bias cut and for creating a fashion for 'Wallis blue' with the wedding dress he designed for the Duchess of Windsor. He opened a salon in New York in 1940. During World War II Mainbocher responded to the problem of fabric rationing by producing short evening dresses and maintaining a restrained, narrow silhouette. He also designed uniforms for WAVES and the American Red Cross, among others.

Maxwell, Vera (Vera Huppé) 1901–. Designer. Born New York, USA. Maxwell started her career by making clothes for herself. By 1936 she was attracting the attention of the fashion press and from the late 1930s her designs were being bought by Seventh Avenue firms such as Adler & Adler. Maxwell established her own business in 1947, creating classic, wearable separates and suits, wraparound jersey

dresses and riding jackets. She was influenced by men's country clothes and used natural dyes to produce autumnal tones.

McCardell, Claire 1905–58. Designer. Born Frederick, USA. McCardell studied at Parsons School of Design in New York, and also in Paris. During the late 1920s and 1930s she worked with Richard Turk at Townley Frocks, and then for Hattie Carnegie. One of her first highly successful designs was the waistless, bias-cut 'monastic dress' of 1938. McCardell returned to Townley Frocks in 1940 to design under her own name, producing easy-fitting clothes which were hugely influential. During the Second World War she responded to the strict rationing of silk and wool with a creative and innovative use of fabrics such as cotton, denim and jersey. Her wraparound 'popover' dress of 1942 became one of her most popular and durable designs.

Molyneux, (Captain) Edward 1891–1974. Designer. Born London, England. Molyneux began his career producing illustrations for magazines and advertisements and in 1911 was employed as a sketcher by Lucile. He opened his own couture house in Paris in 1919, becoming famous for simple tailored suits and skirts in muted tones which were seen as archetypally English in their restrained elegance. Between 1925 and 1932 he opened further branches in Monte Carlo, Cannes, Biarritz and also London, where he continued to work during World War II, producing graceful, streamlined garments. Molyneux retired in 1950. An attempted comeback in 1965 was unsuccessful.

Morton, Digby 1906–83. Designer. Born Dublin, Ireland. After studying art and architecture in Ireland, Morton worked for Lachasse in London in the late 1920s and established his own business in 1933. He became well known for his use of Aran knits and Donegal tweeds often combined with silk blouses. Morton is also widely credited with having adapted the traditional tailor-made suit to make it more graceful and up to date. He created the uniforms for the Women's Voluntary Service in 1939 and in the late 1940s and

1950s produced designs for various US manufacturers.

Norell, Norman (Norman Levinson) 1900–72. Designer. Born Noblesville, USA. From 1922 Norell worked as a costume designer and for the Seventh Avenue firm Charles Armour. In 1928 he joined Hattie Carnegie, where he remained until he founded Traina-Norell with Anthony Traina in 1941. During the 1940s and 1950s Norell made his reputation as one of America's finest designers, known not only for sophisticated, elaborately trimmed eveningwear but also for his fur trenchcoats, sequined sheath dresses, and empire-line dresses. He established his own house in 1960.

Piguet, Robert 1901–53. Designer. Born Yverdon, Switzerland. After training as a banker, Piguet moved to Paris in 1918 and worked for Redfern and Poiret. Opening in 1933, the House of Piguet was known for romantic evening gowns and elegant suits and dresses, often in grey, beige or blue. Piguet also made costumes for the stage and frequently employed other designers, including Balmain, Dior, Galanos and Givenchy.

Rochas, Marcel 1902–55. Designer. Born Paris, France. Rochas established his house in 1924, becoming an influential designer whose work at times heralded styles which became current years later. Inspired by Javanese and Balinese traditional costumes, he introduced broad-shouldered garments to his collections in 1933, creating a look usually attributed to Schiaparelli. Other innovative designs included sculpted wool coats with widely stitched seams, trouser suits in grey flannel and the tight-waisted 'guêpière' corset of 1942 which presaged the more feminine shapes of the 1950s. Rochas was also famous for imaginative embroidery and appliqués and bizarre decorative features such as stuffed birds and buttons shaped like butterflies, lipstick and pipes. He often worked with flower-patterned fabric and was one of the first designers to add pockets to skirts.

Schiaparelli, Elsa 1890–1973. Designer. Born Rome, Italy. Schiaparelli moved to Paris in 1922 and opened a boutique,

'Pour le Sport', in 1927. The following year she showed her first collection. Her clothes were chic and eccentric, strongly influenced by modern art movements. She commissioned artists such as Salvador Dali and Jean Cocteau to design fabrics and accessories and produced a range of surreal garments, often with *trompe-l'oeil* effects. Her many innovations included unusually shaped buttons, padlock fastenings, lip-shaped pockets, and hats in the form of ice-cream cones, shoes or lamb cutlets. In 1933 her broad-shouldered pagoda sleeve set the basic shape for fashion until the New Look. The house of Schiaparelli closed during the war and re-opened in 1945. Known for her gifted use of colour, Schiaparelli promoted 'Shocking Pink' and was the first designer to use plastic zippers decoratively.

Trigère, Pauline 1912–. Designer. Born Paris, France. As a child Trigère helped her mother in her dressmaking business and later worked as a cutter for Martial et Armand. After moving to New York and working for Travis Banton at Hattie Carnegie, she opened her own house in 1942. Trigère achieved instant success with her finely tailored, original designs, often created by draping fabric directly on the model. Among her many innovations were removable scarves and collars, dresses with jewelry attached and reversible coats and capes. She was also known for her use of the bias cut. In the late 1940s Trigère launched a ready-to-wear line.

Valentina (Valentina Nicholaevna Sanina) 1899–1989. Designer. Born Kiev, Russia. Valentina established her house in 1928. She designed costumes for many theatrical productions as well as offstage clothes for actresses, including Katharine Hepburn, Greta Garbo and Gloria Swanson. While her daywear was often simple and practical, sometimes displaying peasant influences, her evening wear and swirling capes were highly dramatic. She was also a skilled designer of millinery, in particular snoods, turbans and veils. During the late 1940s Valentina achieved considerable success with her full ballerina-length skirts worn with ballet slippers.

Sources for 1940s Fashion

Anderson Black, J.
and Madge Garland
A History of Fashion, 1975

Baynes, Ken
and Kate Baynes, eds.
The Shoe Show: British Shoes since 1790, 1979

Bradfield, Nancy
Historical Costumes of England, 1958

Broby-Johansen, R.
Body and Clothes: An Illustrated History of Costume, 1966

Byrde, Penelope
The Male Image: Men's Fashion in England 1300–1970, 1979

Carter, Ernestine
The Changing World of Fashion: 1900 to the Present, 1977

Contini, Mila
Fashion, 1965

Cunnington, C. Willett
English Women's Clothing in the Present Century, 1952

Cunnington, C. Willett
and Phillis Cunnington
The History of Underclothes, 1951

De Courtais, Georgine
Women's Headdress and Hairstyles, 1973

De la Haye, Amy
The Cutting Edge: 50 Years of British Fashion 1947–1997, 1996

De Marly, Diana
Fashion for Men: An Illustrated History, 1985

Dorner, Jane
Fashion in the Forties and Fifties, 1974

Ewing, Elizabeth
Dress and Undress: A History of Women's Underwear, 1978
Fur in Dress, 1981

Gallery of English Costume
Weddings, 1976

Ginsburg, Madeleine
Wedding Dress 1740–1970, 1981
The Hat: Trends and Traditions, 1990

Hall-Duncan, Nancy
The History of Fashion Photography, 1979

Hanson, Henny Harald
Costume Cavalcade, 1956

Harrison, Michael
The History of the Hat, 1960

Howell, Georgina
In Vogue: Six Decades of Fashion, 1975

Jarvis, Anthea
Brides, Wedding Clothes and Customs 1850–1980, 1983

Kennett, Frances
The Collector's Book of Twentieth Century Fashion, 1983

La Vine, W. Robert
In a Glamorous Fashion, 1981

Langley-Moore, Doris
Fashion through Fashion Plates, 1971

Latour, Anny
Kings of Fashion, 1958

Laver, James
Costume, 1963

Laver, James
and Amy de la Haye
Costume and Fashion: A Concise History, 1995

Lee-Potter, Charlie
Sportswear in Vogue, 1984

Lynham, Ruth, ed.
Paris Fashion: The Great Designers and Their Creations, 1972

Martin, Richard
and Harold Koda
Jocks and Nerds: Men's Style in the Twentieth Century, 1989

Mulvagh, Jane
Vogue: History of 20th Century Fashion, 1988

O'Hara, Georgina
The Encyclopaedia of Fashion, 1986

Peacock, John
Fashion Sketchbook: 1920–1960, 1977
Costume 1066 to the 1990s, 1986
The Chronicle of Western Costume, 1991
20th Century Fashion, 1993
Men's Fashion, 1996

Polhemus, Ted
Streetstyle, 1994

Polhemus, Ted
and Lynn Proctor
Fashion and Anti-Fashion: An Anthology of Clothing and Adornment, 1978

Probert, Christina
Lingerie in Vogue since 1910, 1981

Robinson, Julian
Fashion in the Forties, 1976
The Fine Art of Fashion: An Illustrated History, 1989

Saint Laurent, Cecil
The History of Ladies' Underwear, 1968

Simon, Pedro
The Bikini, 1986

Wilcox, R. Turner
The Mode in Costume, 1942
Five Centuries of American Costume, 1963
The Dictionary of Costume, 1969

Yarwood, Doreen
English Costume: From the Second Century to 1967, 1952

Magazines and Journals

Butterick Fashion News, London, 1940–1941

Croquis Couture: Série Robes et Ensembles, Créations Eté, Lyons, 1949

Fashion: Lorraine Fashion Studios, New York, 1949

Fashions and Fabrics, London, 1948–1949

Garment Fashion: Coat and Suit Edition, New York, 1945

Harper's Bazaar, London, 1940–1949

Home Fashions, London, 1940–1945

Glamour, New York, 1948

Illustrated, London, 1948

Les Premiers Dessins, Paris, 1947–1949

Mademoiselle, New York, 1949

Needlework Illustrated, London, 1941–1946

Robes Pratiques: Revue Périodique, Paris, 1949

Sartorial Gazette, London, 1940

Stitchcraft, London, 1940–1943

Vogue, London, 1940–1949

Vogue Pattern Book, London, 1940–1943

Weldon Fashion Series, London, 1940–1945

Woman's Weekly, London, 1947–1949

Acknowledgments

Thanks are due to Janet Dunham, of Zero Antiques Clothes Shop in Newcastle-under-Lyme, for her help and kindness, and for the loan of her many costume magazines.

I also extend my gratitude to the Yale School of Art and Design, Wrexham, Clwyd, for the use of their facilities.